Samuel Wesley, Eliza Wesley

Letters of Samuel Wesley to Mr. Jacobs,

Organist of Surrey Chapel, Relating to the Introduction into this Country of

the Works of John Sebastian Bach. Second Edition

Samuel Wesley, Eliza Wesley

Letters of Samuel Wesley to Mr. Jacobs,
Organist of Surrey Chapel, Relating to the Introduction into this Country of the
Works of John Sebastian Bach. Second Edition

ISBN/EAN: 9783744716666

Printed in Europe, USA, Canada, Australia, Japan

Cover: Foto ©ninafisch / pixelio.de

More available books at **www.hansebooks.com**

LETTERS

OF

SAMUEL WESLEY

TO

MR. JACOBS,

ORGANIST OF SURREY CHAPEL, RELATING TO THE INTRODUCTION INTO THIS
COUNTRY OF THE WORKS OF

JOHN SEBASTIAN BACH.

(NOW FIRST PUBLISHED.)

EDITED BY HIS DAUGHTER

ELIZA WESLEY.

SECOND EDITION.

London:
WILLIAM REEVES, 185, FLEET STREET, E.C.,
Publisher of Musical Works.

1878.

In sending forth to the Musical Public the accompanying Letters of my Father, I am impelled to publish them by a sense of duty to his memory, in order to show that it was to his discernment and zealous perseverance that Bach's transcendent genius was made known and appreciated (although tardily, and through much opposition) by the English Musical World. I refer with pride to the result of his exertions in what he called " the cause of Truth and Justice."

Having Copies of the Letters by me,—now, when Bach's Music is so well known and appreciated,—I have thought it an appropriate time to gratify the long desired wish to publish them, so that the award of " Honour to whom Honour is due" may be inscribed to my Father's memory.

E. W.

May 11th, 1875.

LETTERS.

LETTER I.

DEAR SIR,—I am much obliged by your ingenious and circumstantial Detail of your success with *Saint Sebastian*, as you very properly term him, and am rejoiced to find that you are likely to regard his Works with me as a musical Bible unrivalled and inimitable.

I am grieved to witness in my valuable Friend Doctor Burney's Critique (for he is a man whom I equally respect and love), so slight an acquaintance with the great and matchless Genius whom he professes to analyze : and I have however much satisfaction in being able to assure you, *from my own personal experience*, that his present judgment of our Demi-God is of a very different Nature from that at the Time he imprudently, incautiously, and we may add, *ignorantly* pronounced so rash and false a verdict (although a false Verdict is a contradiction in Terms), as that which I this Day read for the first Time upon "the greatest Master of Harmony in any Age or Country."

It is now I think nearly a twelvemonth since I wrote to the Doctor respecting my profound admiration (and Adoration if you like it as well) of Sebastian : I stated to him that I had made a Study

B

of his Preludes and Fugues, adding that his compositions had opened to me an entirely new musical World, which was to me at least as surprising as (when a child) I was thunderstruck by the opening of the Dettingen Te Deum, at the Bristol Cathedral with about an hundred Performers (a great Band in those Days). I went into something like a general Description of what I conceived to be his characteristic Beauties, and particularly specified *Air* as one of the chief and most striking. I have by me the Doctor's reply to my letter, although I cannot at the present moment advert to it, but I fully remember his observing in nearly the following Words:—" In order to be consistent with myself with regard to the great Sebastian Bach, before I precisely coincide with you, I must refer to what I have written at various Times and in various Places of my History, Travels, &c., in which I had occasion to mention him; but I shall feel exceedingly gratified in hearing his elaborate and erudite Compositions performed by you (for I never yet HEARD any one of them), and can tell you that I have a very curious and beautiful Copy of *his Fugues,* which was presented to me many years since by his Son Emanuel, and which I shall have much pleasure in shewing you."

When I waited on my venerable Friend he had been kind enough to previously lay upon his Music Desk, the MS. in question (together with several other beautiful and superb Works of our immortal Master) ; but when I came to examine this said rare Present, how much was I surprised to find it so full of *scriptural* Faults, that it was not without some Difficulty I could manage to do justice to one of the Fugues which I had been formerly the most familiar with; and although I did not *boggle*, yet I played with extreme Discomfort. My Friend, however, was extremely delighted, and the very first Part of his Critique expressed his Wonder *how such abstruse harmony* and such perfect and enchanting melody could have been so marvellously united!

What a convincing Proof this is, that his *former* criticism upon our matchless Author was an hasty and improvident Step!

I conceive that the Fact stands thus : When Burney was in Germany, the universal Plaudits and Panegyricks upon the Father of *universal Harmony* were so interesting that it would have been impossible for him to have avoided giving such a Man a Place in his Account of Musical Authors in his General History : Nevertheless it appears very evidently from the erroneous Sentence he has pronounced therein upon the Comparative Merit of him and Handel, that he never could have taken due Pains to make himself Master of the Subject, other. wise his late candid acknowledgement would not have been made, and is proof sufficient that he only wanted *experience* of the *Truth* to make him ready and willing to own it.

I must also tell you another Piece of News;— namely that this imperfect and incorrect volume, this *valuable* and inestimable Gift of Sebastian's dutiful Son, happens to contain only the 24 *first* Preludes and Fugues; all written in the Soprano

Clef (to make them more easily understood, I suppose), and the Preludes so miserably mangled and mutilated that had I not met them in such a collection as that of the learned and highly illuminated Doctor Burney, I verily believe that I should have exclaimed, " An Enemy hath done this." I should have at once concluded that such a manuscript could have been made only by him who was determined to disgrace instead of promote the cause of correct Harmony.

Ever since I had the privilege of so great a triumph (for I can call it nought else) over the Doctor's Prejudice, he has evinced the most cordial veneration for our Sacred Musician, and when I told him that I was in Possession of 24 *more* such precious Relicks, he was all aghast in finding that there could be any Productions of such a Nature which he had not seen : this again is another proof of his having hastily judged, and also how remiss the Germans must have been not to have made him better acquainted with the Works of their transcendant Countryman.

I am told by the Rev. Mr. Picart (one of the Canons of Hereford Cathedral) that Seb. B. has written Pieces for *three* Organs, and innumerable others, which are not sent to England purely from the contempt which the Germans entertain of the general state of Music in this Country, and which unfavourable sentiment I am sorry to say has but too much foundation on the Truth.

You see that there are others who have as much cause to apologize for the length of Letters as you, if apology were at all necessary among Friends; but yours which I this Day received has given me so much real satisfaction, as I fully trust that you are determined to defend the cause of Truth and Sebastian (for they are one) against all the frivolous objections of Ignorance, and the transparent Cavils of Envy, that I safely rely upon you as one of my right hand men against all the prejudiced Handelians. It has been said that Comparisons are odious; but without Comparison, where is Discrimination? and without Discrimination, how are we to attain a just judgment? Let us always weigh fairly as far as human Powers will allow, and endeavour to divest ourselves of the Propensity which leads us either to idolize or execrate whatever we have been unfortunately habituated so to do without previous and due examination.

I feel great gratification in having been *accessory* to your study of Sebastian: I know that you had only to know him to love and adore him and I sincerely assure you that in meeting so true an Enthusiast in so good a Cause (and depend on it that nothing very good or very great is done without enthusiasm), I experience a warmth of Heart which only enthusiasts know or can value.

That our *Friendship* may long continue, either with or without enthusiasm (tho' I think a spice of it even there no bad thing), believe me, is the very cordial wish of, Dear Sir,

Yours very faithfully,

LETTER II.

To Mr. Jacobs,

Charlotte Street, Black Friars Road.
October 17th, 1808.

My dear Sir,—We are going on swimmingly. Mr. Horn (the Music Master to the Princesses) is furthering the cause of our grand Hero with might and main. He had arranged 12 of the Fugues for 4 Instruments before I had the pleasure of his Acquaintance, and was longing to find some spirited enthusiast like himself to co-operate in bringing the Musical World to Reason and Common Sense, and to extort a Confession of the true State of the Case against the Prepossession, Prejudice, Envy, and Ignorance of all Anti-Bachists.

We are (in the first place) preparing for the Press an authentic and accurate Life of Sebastian, which Mr. Stephenson the Banker (a most zealous and scientific member of our Fraternity) has translated into English from the German of Forkel, and wherein is a list of *all* the Works of our Apollo.

This we propose to publish by subscription as a preparatory measure to editing the Fugues, and which will naturally cause a Considerable Sensation, not only in the Musical but also in the Literary World.—Is not this all as you would have it? I cannot doubt your affirmative, and you perceive that I have not been idle.

It appears by the Life of Sebastian, he was not

only the greatest Master in the World, but also one of the most worthy and amiable Characters that ever adorned Society. I remember often exclaiming when working at him, " I am sure that none but a *good* man could have written thus ;" and you perceive that my conjecture was accurate.

Mr. Horn has a vast quantity of his Compositions that have never seen the light; among the rest, Stupendous Trios for the Organ, which he used to play thus : his right hand played the first part on the Top Row of the Clavier ; his left the 2nd Part on the 2nd Row, and he played the Bass *wholly* upon the Pedals. There are Allegro Movements among them, and occasionally very brisk notes in the Bass Part, whence it appears that he was alike dexterous both with hands and feet.

Horn has a further Design than the mere Publication of our 48 Preludes and Fugues ; he wishes to extend the Work to a Complete Edition of all his Compositions that are to be found ; and if God spare our Health, why should we despair of presenting the world with "all these Treasures of Wisdom and Knowledge ?"

He is as indefatigable as yourself, and has written with his own hand whole centuries of Pages which would amaze you. He has not only transcribed all the 48 Preludes and Fugues, but also written them on paper ruled for the purpose, capacious enough to contain an *entire Fugue* however long, upon two pages only, thus avoiding the Inconvenience of turning over, for which there is hereby no necessity even from the beginning of the Work to the end.

Mr. Kollman in his essay on practical Musical Composition, 1799, has published one of those Trios above mentioned, towards the end of the musical examples (N 58); by this you will be able to judge of the rest; for there is no Inferiority throughout them; all are equally admirable and excellent, altho' each in an entirely different style.

I sadly want to see you, tho' I know not well how to contrive it. St. Paul's opens again on Sunday next and I have promised Attwood to look in there in the morning. In what part of the same Day should I be most like to find you?

Yours ever truly,

I know not Mr. Neate's correct address; will you therefore be so kind as to forward the enclosed to him immediately?

Do not forget my kind regards to my Friend Mrs. Jacobs.

LETTER III.

MY DEAR SIR,—l thought you would be gratified in
gaining early intelligence of our intention to come
forward with Memoirs of our matchless Man (if
Man he may be called), as I am clearly of Opinion
that they will serve as a thorough defiance of all
the Snarlers and would-be Criticks, howsoever
dispersed throughout the British Empire. Upon the
Continent his fame has been so long circulated and
established, that they must have for many years past
sneered at our Ignorance of such an Author, pro-
fessing (as we do) to be a Nation attached to Music.
Saloman has said, truly and shrewdly enough, that
the English know very little of the Works of the
German Masters, Handel excepted, who (as he
observes) came over hither when there was a great
dearth of good Musick, and here he remained (these
are his words) establishing a Reputation wholly
Constituted *upon the Spoils of the Continent.*

This would nettle the Handelians devilishly; however it is the strict truth, for we all know how he
has pilfered from all manner of Authors whence he
could filch anything like a Thought worth embodying;
and although it is certain that what he had taken
he has generally improved on (not when he robbed
the Golden Treasury of Sebastian by the way), yet
there is such a meanness in putting even his own

subjects in so many different Works over and over again, vide his Lessons, Concertos, Chamber Duets, Instrumental Trios, and almost all his Compositions, that I do sincerely think, and am ready to maintain it among sensible unprejudiced Judges. (For it is but Time lost to argue with Bigots, which is another word for Madmen.) Handel, for so great a Master, has as little just claim to the merit of original genius as the most servile of his Imitators.

I am glad you tickled up Gaffer Stevens a bit: I need not tell you that half, and more than half, even of such Professors as ought to know and do know better, give a decision hap-Hazard upon sundry matters which they have never duly considered. I am delighted that you happened to remember Burney's identical words : your anticipation of what he was about to say must have been not an agreeable surprize, but rather of the confounding kind ! Just while I think of it, let me provide you with immediate ammunition against the feeble defence of Handel upon the score of his *clear and marked* Subjects. The Doctor's Fugue you have accurately, as also the Judgment Fugue, and what I call the Saints-in-Glory Fugue, by which I mean that in E. Major, four sharps.

Add to this the one hard by it in E flat Major, and I think these will furnish sufficient for many *Rounds* against such as " love darkness rather than light, because their Eyes and Ears are evil."

However, as I before observed to you, History and experience teach us, that the Progress of Truth, however slow, is always infallibly sure. How many hundreds have been regarded as Hereticks and Atheists (and treated accordingly), for maintaining that *the Earth turns round*, and now, who but Savages and Idiots believe the contrary ?

The affair is this : a great Majority of those who exist or at least derive Emolument by teaching and governing others, are themselves very incompetent to either : it is natural that they should dread the Detection of their Ignorance, since, as was said of old, " it is by this Craft they get their Gain."

You may rely on it that you yourself are looked upon with a thorough envious Eye by your Brother Organists, who instead of endeavouring successfully to imitate your persevering Industry, by which you have accomplished so much, and gained such a clear Insight into the true Style of our Author, prefer the shorter and easier Way (as they think) of establishing their Pretentions to Criticism by defaming their Superiors.

Your letter found me this Evening in my Chamber, to which I have been confined all Day, or rather from which I dreaded to go out, having had a severe Touch of a bilious Complaint, to which I am occasionally subject, particularly at this Time of the year : but a Day's nursing and a few grains of Rhubarb and Magnesia, or the like, almost always set me to Rights again, and I fully expect to get out To-morrow, of which indeed I should much regret to be disappointed, as I am engaged to a Party where we are to have some of Sebastian, arranged by Horn, for 2 violins, Tenor and Bass, and a glorious effect they produce, as you may guess. What must they do in a full Orchestra ! ?

Even Germans themselves are not free from the Envy of such a transcendant Genius.

I will not tell you the name of the Person till Sunday (for I mean to be with you), neither would you *believe*, and perhaps can hardly credit it on my solemn Asseveration, that a Man of real musical judgment, some science, and admirable Talent on his own Instrument, compared one of those Fugues which Horn has arranged (which you do not remember as not among the 48), to *a Hog floundering in the Mud.*

Thank Heaven that Prejudice and Spite, however prevalent in England, are not solely found here : if it were so, I should wish rather to be ranked among the honest Hindoo Barbarians.

Adieu. I trust to see you on Sunday, by 1 o'clock.

Yours ever truly,

S. Wesley

Mrs. W. joins in best wishes to Mrs. J., yourself, and Family.

LETTER IV.

To Mr. Jacobs,

Charlotte Street, Black Friars Road.
November 17th, 1808.

My DEAR SIR,—I always suspect the sincerity of sudden Conversions. Had not my Brother known of your intimate Acquaintance with me, I should have been sooner induced to think that his Heart and his Words went together on Monday Night; but as I know he *can* play Saloman's Tricks (if not upon the Fiddle, yet upon a more dangerous Instrument described by St. James), I own I am a little of the Sadducee in the present Instance, and am really afraid that (in regard to my Brother's real opinion of Bach) " there is no Resurrection."

I have already repeatedly expressed to you my regret that a Man of my Brother's very transcendant Musical knowledge and skill, should have been so betrayed *by bad Company into* Habits of thinking and acting so diametrically opposite to his convictions and better judgement : of course it follows (and I am sure that *you* will give me credit for it), that whatever I have said, or ever shall say which may have an appearance of severity cannot be the result of any worse Principle than the *Grief,* not the *Anger,* I feel in the Perversion and Perversity of such a mind.

Well then you will not suppose that in what I speak to you Confidentially, concerning C. W., I

have either "Envy, Hatred, Malice, or Uncharitable-
ness." The Searcher of all Hearts knoweth the
contrary : I think of him with some pleasure as to
the *native* and *original* Goodness of his disposition
but with more melancholy when I consider such a
Cruel Sacrifice to the whims and Artifices of design-
ing Persons, who have made him the mere Puppet
of their base and interested Designs.

Now to more pleasing Reflexions.—I am glad that
you brought forward the Hymn Tune for two
Reasons, the former (and the better), because I know
it is just in the style which particularly pleases C. W.
(for his best Compositions are pathetic) : and 2dly.
if he should venture to report the fact to our worthy
Sister she will be extraordinarily chagrined in finding
that a man whom she has represented (these are her
own Words) as "destitute of every Sentiment of
Justice, Honour, or Integrity," should have had
sufficient Respect to any religious Words to think of
setting them to Music : I dare say she will add that
they are thoroughly profaned by the experiment.

Your playing Bach on Monday set my Brother
upon his *Battle-Horse.* I'll answer for it that he
made Handel's Harmonies tolerably full—I never
yet found any other man who seemed so *made* for
him—Kelway, C.W.'s Harpsichord Master (an admirable Musician and perfect Player), was known to
have said that W. played Handel in a vastly superior
manner even to Handel himself.—Kelway (by the
Way) was one of the most accurate Criticks of
Performance of his (or perhaps any other) Time.

I can have no possible objection to acceding to

your request about sitting to Mr. Bacon, but would wish to know how long at one Time he would require my Attendance: it will be extremely agreeable to me to be better acquainted with him, and I wish you to signify the same to him your first convenient Opportunity. If he will give me legal Notice, by which I mean about the space of a week, I will wait upon him with much Pleasure; we can then settle a Time for my sitting to him, which I do not think would suit me on any day when I go to Cossens's, as I am always full of crowded Work then from Morning till Night.

Pray inform Mr. G. Gwilt that I shall with great satisfaction, attend him on Wednesday; I must Cut and Contrive how to Manage, for this is my Paddington Day, and I must be Cunning to *transfer* some of the business on the occasion. I fear there is no possibility of getting previously to your Organ, because it will be no easy matter for me to get into your Latitude sooner than ½ past 4, and even then I must beg leave to attend the Brats at a much earlier hour than usual in order to accomplish this.

You may also tell Elliott that I will dine with him on some Day between the 20th and 27th as desired, altho' I do not love "a little Church Organ."

Perhaps this is only an Antiphrasis, and that he and you mean a great one.

Remember me in the kindest way to

Mrs.  and all my young Bachists, and I trust that I shall remain (not only in this, but in a better World)

Your lasting Friend,

LETTER V.

Nov. 22, 1808.

MY DEAR SIR,—Although I fully hope and expect to enjoy your Company on Wednesday next, yet as you ask me a question in your last concerning a Personage who (as you very truly observe) is an acquisition to any Musical Cause that he is determined to espouse, I am pleased in an opportunity of coinciding with you upon so agreeable a subject, as a candid confession proceeding from a mind formerly prejudiced, but now (I trust) conquered by the irresistible Omnipotence of Truth.

You ask me what I think—I think with you that my Brother held out as long as he could but that being so closely besieged by very many Judges of Music who have been so thoroughly and sincerely converted to the Truth of the *Bach Perfection*, he found it impossible to maintain a tenable Post any longer, and therefore wisely made a virtue of Necessity, for I am yet of Opinion that if he could even now defend the Pre-eminence of Handel he would; and I have but little doubt (so long and so well as I have known him) that amongst mere Handelians he will but too readily relapse into Blasphemy.

Now observe that I do not say this as if I were indifferent on which side he enlisted, but am only endeavouring to prove to you from my own experience that you will do well not to be too implicit in your Faith with regard to his *real* Opinion. There can be no question that *while he is hearing* the Sublimities of our Idol, he must prefer them to any other Sounds that could have been conceived; but no sooner does a Temptation to his *besetting* Sin (the blind Worship of Handel) fall in his way, than he returns to his " wallowing in the mire."

Time proves all Things, and I sincerely hope (tho' I much doubt) that it may prove my conjectures erroneous.

On Wednesday we may appoint a day for Mr. Bacon, and on Saturday I will somehow or other endeavour to manage a meeting at Elliott's. The fact is, that Saturday is one of my Paddington Days, and there is that Nuisance in Society yclept a Dancing Master who usurps my Territory till 1 o'clock, and I have always 4 hours' work after him. The Governess is not among the most accommodating of her sex, and often gives herself more airs than I can very patiently tolerate. Although upon occasion I can be a Match for saucy people, yet as Litigation always puts me in a Fever (which is a dear Sacrifice for Victory), I would rather prevent Dispute than exert my power of Defence. We will, however, talk this over thoroughly on Wednesday, or rather perhaps on Thursday Morning, for I shall make use of my Blanket Privilege in Charlotte Street on the preceding night, unless any circumstance in your domestic Arrangements may possibly render it inconvenient. With regard to Lyne's Primer Grammar, I can take it with me when I next part from you. Charles is quite overjoyed in anticipating the utility of which I know it will be to him even *now*, after having waded through Lilly's.

The Method is beautifully simple, and I am persuaded that with *your* Application (which I know not a parallell unto, excepting in John Cramer and Sir Isaac Newton) I am persuaded that all the Latin you will find occasion for you will acquire within a few months. I have changed my form of salutation this time. Pray remember me most kindly to

Mrs.  &c.

Adieu,

LETTER VI.

Camden Town,
Thursday, December 8th, 1808.

My DEAR SIR,—Previously to the receipt of your
last kind letter which I this day received, I had resolved to have nothing to do with that infamous
Libeller the Satyrist : for any Person either of
decent character or tolerable Education to contend
with such a Wretch would be about as wise as
for a General to send a formal Challenge to a
Scavenger.

I was informed to Day that I am to expect a
Summons from a friend to a grand Birth Day Anni-
versary Dinner on the 21st. However, as it has
not yet arrived, I shall consider myself previously
engaged to you and Mr. Bacon, therefore I hereby
commission you to convey my respects to him, and
if 6 o'clock should not be too late for him (as I
cannot get loose from the Manor House till ½ past 5),
I will hope for the Pleasure of joining your Party.

I am glad to find that Sebastian is to be heard
even " out of the Mouths of Babes and Sucklings " :
depend on it there is nothing more necessary to
render his divine Strains the Chief delight and solace
of all *truly harmonized* Souls, but an assiduous culti-
vation of them. He was certainly dropped down
among us from Heaven.

I am concerned to find that your Friend αγωνιζομενος
is not likely to domesticate among us, but yet am

c 2

rejoiced to find there are hopes of at least a transient visit.

He certainly is a very superior man, and as such men are scarce, I am indeed idolatrously covetous of such society. I am happy in being able to declare that I feel myself supported by the Friendship (the best *human* Prop) of a little Phalanx of such characters as I do think I may venture to say were "made only a little lower than the Angels," and what I most fear is that the Kindness I experience in this World will render me too fond of it, and make me mistake Earth for Heaven.

I am much flattered by the good opinion which your venerable Friend is pleased to entertain of me, although I have afforded him no *practical* Proof of deserving it, unless in the exercise of my Fingers. I assure you that I have not felt so much affected by any Harangue from the Pulpit for many years past as I was on Sunday by the honest unstudied natural discourse Mr. Hill gave us :* I prefer such a sermon to all the polished rhetorical essays in the World, which (most falsely) are called *Preaching* : moralizing is the utmost extent of the Term suitable to such cold, dry, lifeless Compositions, and I had rather hear two pages of John Bunyan's Pilgrim than Folios of such uninteresting trash.

N.B. I had rather be your joint Organist than your Successor, although I am very grateful to Mr. Hill for his thinking me worthy the latter post : I trust that (if it be best for us) we may live for some

---

* Rev. Rowland Hill, A.M.

years yet to be mutually serviceable, for the cause of Music, Friendship, and of Truth, which I am old-fashioned enough to think ought never to be separated; and in the love of the Truth believe me,

My dear Sir, yours faithfully,

Mrs. W. unites with us all in kindest regards.

LETTER VII.

To MR. JACOBS,
Charlotte Street, Black Friars Road.

Camden Town,
March 2nd, 1809.

MY DEAR SIR,—Here I am once more, and shall rejoice in the first Opportunity afforded me of an Interview after so long an Interval of Separation. You will, I know, give me full Credit for not having intentionally neglected writing to you; believe me I have been a greater slave *during the Holidays* than I am when in the Mill-Horse Road of A B C Drudgery, hurried and dragged about from Pillar to Post, and at Times when I most wanted and needed Retirement and quiet for preparing my first Lecture, which although not designed for a profound or very luminous Composition (which I assure you *bona*

Fide that it will not be) yet some previous Meditation was needful, were it only to make a string of Trifles of the same *Tissue ;* for nothing you know can be less tolerable than the mere outward and visible Sign of a Discourse, without any of the inward and Spiritual Grace that ought to attend it. As matters have turned out I am all in good time. My first Lecture, such as it is, has been in Readiness for some Days, and I think I have no very Contemptible Skeletons prepared for a second and third, which will make up *half* the course. I also think that I have at least a good *Subject* for a 4th if not a 5th, and if the miracles of Sebastian will not furnish me Ammunition for a 6th I must have rather changed my faith in him.—By the way I have had the Loan of many *exercises* of his for the Harpsichord, which are every Whit as stupendous as the Preludes and Fugues, and demonstrate him (what every fresh scrap of his I meet with does) the very quintessence of all Musical Excellence.

It's droll enough, that amongst these is inserted a beautiful Air which is published along with a sett of Emanuel Bach's Lessons, and which I saw at Bath : I am very much inclined to think that this Son, like many others, made but little scruple of robbing his Father ; and that he was not concerned for his Honour seems plain enough by the vile and most diabolical Copy that he gave Dr. Burney as a Present, and from which the latter was wise enough to judge of and damn his Works (as he thought), but the Phœnix must always revive.

I assure you I have long wished to be again among my London Friends, and am not a little revived by feeling myself in the old saddle again, hard as I must travel ; for *new* Friends, however kind and sincere they may eventually prove, have not the *mellow* effect upon the Mind (if I may so say) as older ones, and it takes some time to study People's Habits and Inclinations before we can be in that perfectly pleasant Familiarity in their Conversation which to me is the most delicious Point in Society. I trust that my good Friend and generous Hostess, whose name I need not mention, is in good Health, whom I assure you I mean to visit before long, whether you are in the Way or not, so now you have legal Notice, and may take your measures Accordingly. As my Lecture is not to be read before next Friday Week (by the Request of one of the Governors who cannot attend on the Wednesday before, as I had appointed, and who do me the Honor to wish to be present), I shall be able, by Hook or by Crook to see you and have a Pennyworth of Chat upon the Fun some Day or other between now and then.— I am given to imagine that the *Squad* (you know whom I mean) had rather that their old Friend the Devil were Lecturer than I.

Yours very truly,

Remember me to Rowley and all the young Powlies.

LETTER VIII.

To Mr. Jacobs,
Charlotte Street, Black Friars Road.

Camden Town,
March 3, 1809.

My DEAR SIR,—I have just received your very prompt Answer to mine, and regret much that I am unable to be with you either To-morrow or Sunday, but I think that if Wednesday next would suit, I could manage to get to you by five o'clock, though I fear not sooner. I wish as speedy a Line as you can give me on the Subject.

To your Query respecting Sebastian I at once reply in the Affirmative; his Works would furnish Materials for six hundred as easily as for six Lectures, and were all or half which he has written to be critically analysed, and only animadverted upon, I doubt much whether the longest Life would not prove too short for the Task.

But we must for the present confine and repress our Inclination to publish *too hastily* our Creed in the transcendant Merits of this Marvellous Man; it will all go on well by slow degrees, and the Instance you give of Stevens's beginning to revoke his Blasphemies may be considered as a very strong and extraordinary proof of it.

I am glad you like Linley; he is a great Favourite of mine, and indeed I should be peculiarly ungrateful were I not attached to him, as I have every Reason to think his Regard very sincere;—he

is a Man of much musical Talent, as I dare say you
soon discovered. I have not forgotten having left
your Book of Bach's Lutheran Hymns at John Cramer's House; I will get them back at the first Opportunity; I was reminded particularly of the circumstance two Days ago when I found a Trio or two
among the Exercises which I immediately remembered
having played with you from your own Book. I am
about to put the *First Trio* of the Six lent me by
Horn into the Engraver's Hands almost immediately
—the best Way will be unquestionably to print them
singly.

Remember me very cordially to Mrs. J. and all the
young Fry—all here join in kind respects with,

>> Dear Sir,

>>> Yours ever sincerely,

S Wesley

LETTER IX.

April 26th, 1809.

My DEAR SIR,—I am a great Fool. I forgot whether I desired you to bring with you To-morrow my
two Books of Bach—whether I did or not let me now
request you to bear it in mind. I do *not* forget that

your Choral Vorspiele is (or ought to be) in Cramer's Possession; but rather than you should be *bilked* out of it, you should have my copy to all Perpetuity if there were never another in the *Varsel* World. I hope and expect an happy Day To-morrow; but "who knoweth what a Day may bring forth?" How every Hour proves that "in the midst of Life we are in Death!" but it is well we are assured of whom we may seek for Succour.

Sermonizing having become now a part of my Profession, I will make no Apology for what some of the fine Bloods and Bucks would call Canting; but you and I know better Things: I have much to say to you, but I fear that there will be but little Time to-morrow to talk, save and except with our Fingers.

To-morrow I will bring the Vorspiele if it be only to electrify my Brother with

8 *Ped.*

The Portuguese Fun is not settled yet.

We will give all the stiff Handelians and Wolfians a Death Wound to their Prejudice and their Impudence, or there is no Truth in

LETTER X.

To Mr. Jacobs,

Charlotte Street, Black Friars Road.

Camden Town,
July 24th, 1809.

My DEAR SIR,—The Reverend Canon Picart hath
a most unhappy Mode of endeavouring to explain
himself, but if we can make him out together (and it
is not always two Laymen that are a Match for one
Priest), we may think ourselves luckier than if we
lived in the Times when one Priest could get 100
Laymen burnt without *Benefit of Clergy.*

Our modern Melchisedech writeth thus: "I am
sorry my confused expressions have occasioned you so
much Trouble. I meant Paper ruled with Scores of
Six Staves, or Scores of four Staves in a Page. This
Arrangement I thought would cover Scores of any
Number of Staves from Six to three." He means, I
think, *a Score* of 6 or 4 Staves *as often repeated* in one
Page as the Length or Breadth of the Paper will
admit.

What think you? My dear Mr. Jacobs, this is very
cheap Paper I do own, but it costs a dear deal of
Trouble to write upon it. The Ink will not penetrate
all I can do, and as to the present Sheet, I know and
admit that it is greasy, though from what cause I
know not (*vide* the Top of this and the last Page). I,
however, shall find good Account in employing it upon
other Occasions, although not for writing Letters,

either of Ceremony or Friendship;—the former ought to be written *fair* and the latter *fast*—and I defy any Man to do either one or the other upon this.

Yet it is useful Paper; it is good for making a Memorandum of a Debt to one's Tallow Chandler, or one's Butcher, which one would rather do *at Leisure*, and for which greasy Paper is not ill-calculated, when we consider the above Professions.

I have been so put out of Humour by two or three vexations and impudent Things, news of which I re-received when I returned to Day, that I was glad to have an Opportunity of getting into a less Saturnine Vein by the circumstance afforded me by our Sacerdotal Bachist Picart of assuring you again how truly I am   Ever yours,

LETTER XI.

My DEAR SIR,—I do not profess myself to be so great a Schemer as our late Friend Dr. Arnold, who we all know speculated himself into Mischief too often;

but I have a Plan to propose to you of which I should be glad to have your early Opinion.

It is manifest that Sebastian makes that sort of Sensation which will in a short Time form a *Party* business among several Societies among musical Pretenders; of those who know and like Nobody but Handel, others who swear in only Haydn's, Mozart's, and Beethoven's Works—others who relish only "little Peggy's Love," "A Smile and a Tear," and similar Sublimities, of which you need not be reminded.

Now I really think that all those who have the Courage to speak out in Defence of the greatest of all Harmonists ought to coalesce and amalgamate in a mode which should render their cordial Sentiments and Judgment *unequivocal* in the Face of the World, and that we ought to stigmatize such Hypocrites as affect to be enchanted with Sebastian on one Day and on the next endeavour to depreciate and vilify him.

In order to ascertain who are verily and indeed " The Israelites in whom is no guile," I can think of nothing more expedient than the Formation of a junto among ourselves, composed of Characters who sincerely and conscientiously admit and adhere to the superior excellence of the great Musical High Priest; and who will bend their Minds to a Zealous Promotion of advancing the Cause of Truth and Perfection.

Such a Society would *at least* produce one happy effect, that of rendering *thoroughly* Public what as yet is but partially so. I look upon the State of Music in this Country to be very similar to the State of the Roman Church when the flagrant Abuses and Enormities had arisen to such a Height as to *extort* a Reformation. We know what Wonders were wrought by the Resolution and Perseverance of a single Friar, and that Martin Luther having *Truth* for his firm Foundation (for this was the Reason of his Success) managed in a very short Time to shake the whole Fabric of Ignorance and Superstition, although sanctioned by the Precedence of many former Ages, and enforced by the most despotic Authority both ecclesiastical and civil.

It is high Time that *some* Amendment should take place in the Republic of Musick, and I know of no engine equally powerful with the immortal and adamantine Pillars of Sebastian's Harmony. I really think that our constant and unremitted question to *all* who call themselves Friends to excellence should be " Who is on our side—who ?" And I have but little Doubt that by the Establishment of a *regular Society* in Defence of the Truth, we should ere long reap some good Fruits of our laudable endeavours.

Write me your Thoughts on the Subject as soon as convenient.

Believe me, my dear Sir,

Ever truly yours,

LETTER XII.

MY DEAR SIR,—I omitted to observe to you either on Saturday or Sunday that I am all aground for Music Paper, and I was not wise enough to take down the Direction to the Person from whom you procure that necessary Article to us Minstrels, so good and so cheap. If you should have an Opportunity of soon going that Way, and will kindly bear my present Distress in Remembrance, you will do me a real Benefit, for I want to compleat the Parts of my Concerto without Delay, that I may have nothing else to do but pack up my Awls and whirl away to Tamworth at the appointed Time.

I have just received a letter from Dr. Burney, an extracted Portion of which will not be uninteresting to you. "I believe Mr. Salamon is now out of Town; but when I saw him last, in talking of our *great Sebastian*, he said you were in Possession of some Sonatas of his *divine Manufacture*, with a very fine Violin Part to them which he wished me to hear. I have no Violin in Order; but when I return home († Dr. B. is now at Bulstrod, the seat of the Duke of Portland),† and you are both at Leisure, I wish you would prevail on him to fix a Day, and to send one of his own Violins any time before 2 o'clock; while you are charming me with two Parts, I shall act in a Triple Capacity and play the parts of Pit, Box, and Gallery in rapturously applauding the Composition and Performance."

You see one is never too old to learn, and here is an instance that it is never too late to mend!

What more could the Dr. have said, even had he originally been the like Enthusiast with ourselves in the Cause of Truth.

His *Repentance* (tho' he does not profess it yet in Words) seems so evident from the *zealous* Expressions he uses, that I really think we must cordially forgive the past, for we can hardly expect him when tottering over the Grave, and having attained (whether justly or otherwise) a Reputation for Musical Criticism, publickly to revoke what he advanced at so distant a Period of Time, and when perhaps he thinks that his Strictures are forgotten, or at least overbalanced by his present Acknowledgement of the real State of the Fact.

As soon as I can command an Hour, I will set about my deliberate Opinion on the *various* and inimitable excellencies of THE MAN, which I think will settle the Business at least as decisively as our Challenge to J—ACK P—UDDING.

Adieu for the present,—we must Contrive one more Pull at Surry before I hyke over to Staffordshire.

Kindest Regards to all from
Your Sincere Friend,

J. P.

Tho' J. P. refuses to give up his Name
To muffle his Malice a Hood in,
The matter amounts to exactly the same,
For his Nonsense proclaims 'tis J-ack P-udding.

LETTER XIII.

To Mr. Jacobs,
Charlotte Street, Black Friars Road.
25th Sept.

Birmingham, Monday, 25 Sept., 1809.

My DEAR SIR,—I have the Comfort of acquainting
you that my Tamworth Excursion has proved most
unexpectedly serviceable to my *corporal* Sensations,
for I have been on the mending order ever since my
Arrival there, and I am now in very good Condition at
the Place above dated, whence, however, I must set
out To-morrow morning, and I mean to Travel in the
Oxford two Day Coach, to prevent over Fatigue,
which I was obliged to submit to in the first Instance,
from the Necessity of going at *Night*, which constantly
disagrees with me; and if you remember the Wea-
ther on Monday Night last (or rather Tuesday Morning), you must know that the Situation of Coach
Travellers, whether inside or out, could not be over
and above eligible, especially as we were troubled with
a restless Companion, who was continually jerking
the Windows up and down for what he called *Air*,

D

but which was a furious wind and pelting Rain, so that it was next to a Miracle I did not take a Cold *for the Winter*, but yet I escaped, to my no small surprize.

You will wish to hear how the Performances were received; and I wish you had been among us to have witnessed the Delight they afforded to the whole Audience, who (when at the Church) seemed to long for the Privilege of clapping and rattling their Sticks; even as it was, there was a constant Hum of Applause at the conclusion of every Piece, and there never could have been more strict and flattering Attention any where than was manifest throughout the whole.

The Choruses went off *spank* slap bang, like a Cannon, or Mr. Congreve's Rockets.

Notwithstanding I sat at a great Disadvantage, for the New Choir Organ completely obstructed all possibility of seeing any Part of the Orchestra, but a Violin or two on my right and left Wing, so we were obliged to have a Mirror in Order that I might see Frank Cramer, as it was *just as well* that he and I should start together, and this was managed pretty well, save and except that the necessity of hanging the Glass so high proved a sad annoyance to my unfortunate Neck, which was obliged to stretch till I thought I should never be able to reduce it to its common Length again.

The Concerto was excessively praised, and the Fugue of our Sebastian produced a glorious effect with the Instruments.

I promised Buggins to conduct his Concert here (at Birmingham), which was very well attended at

the Theatre, and the Fantazia I played on the Piano
Forte I concluded with "Roly Poly Gammon and
Spinach," which tickled the Tobies of the Button
Makers at such a rate that I thought I never should
have gotten off the Stage, at least till I had broken
my Back with Bowing. The noise was absolutely
confounding, and if I had not that valuable stock of
Impudence belonging to me, of which you have had
numerous Demonstrations, the weight of the Welcome
must have overpowered my Nerves, and I really
think that even such a Jack-Gentlewoman as Mother
Storace would have been tempted to make a thorough
Faint away of it.

I long to see all our Sebastian Squad, and I trust
we shall soon meet. Remember me most kindly to
all yours, and tell Mrs. Jacobs that even the Brums
are beginning to venerate our Orpheus: at Tamworth the effect of the Fugue among the Orchestra
was such, that they were perpetually humming the
Subject whenever I met any of them in the Streets,
either by Day or by Night.

Adieu, my good Friend.

Excuse this hasty Rhapsody, but I knew you
would accept in good Part any rough hewn Pot-
hooks and Hangers from your very sincere and

Cordial Mess Mate,

Wesley

LETTER XIV.

My DEAR SIR,—Enclosed is the Card I promised. I trust that you will manage (by Hook or by Crook) to look in at the Surry on Tuesday Evening, as altho' the principal Body of the first Lecture is an old Story to you who have both heard and read it, yet I have added two or three Touches I think for the better, and of which I should like to have your Opinion. I shall find my Way to the Lock-up House after I have finished my Sermon, when we will confabulate all how and about *a—many Things*, especially upon your Party at the Chapel, and the immediate pro-mulgation of THE MAN (which expression I now pre-fer to any Epithet of " great " or " wonderful," &c., which are not only common, but *weak*, as is every other Epithet applied to one whom none can suffi-ciently praise).

My Services to the Scarlet W. of Babylon To-Day were very gratefully and handsomely received.

If the Roman Doctrines were like the Roman *Music* we should have Heaven upon Earth.

Yours in haste,

Ever truly,

Wesley

LETTER XV.

To Mr. Jacobs,
Charlotte Street, Black Friars Road.

Friday, 2.

My dear Sir,—I wish your Opinion of delivering to each Person *who presents a* Ticket one of the Cards announcing the Trios of Bach : I should conceive that Mr. Hill could not urge any objection against this, and that it is almost too trifling a Circumstance to render a Consultation upon it *with him* necessary. However, as you know his *ins* and *outs* so much better than I, the matter is left to your decision. I will bring with me a good jolly Lot of the said Cards To-morrow, which at all events will be in as good (or a better) Train of Distribution than when facing Primrose Hill, as at present.

I think there can be no question that the Circulation of them on Wednesday would push on the Cause of the Trios Materially. I have not sent M. P. King a Notice of Wednesday and will leave it to you. I have exhausted all the Ammunition brought by your Messenger, and have sent to Hoare, Wright, and some other Bankers of Consequence (Hammersley for Instance), all of whom are musical, and will *prate* about the Thing, which you know is all we want at present : and if a Majority happen to be pleased (which we may without much Presumption conclude) we shall have no bad chance

of being *paid* for our Work at a future Opportunity.
I think if you can borrow a *Court Guide,* or List of
Lords, Ladies, Bucks, and other Blackguards, we
may meet with a few Names that we shall be
unwilling to have omitted when the grand Day is
over.

I long to know what you have written to my
Brother, and whether you have given him a coaxing
Word or two. I fear that setting J. S. B. before
G. F. H., will in spite of all good endeavours on your
Part, be regarded as an unpardonable Sin.

I believe that no *Lecture on Prejudice* will ever
eradicate his. What a grievous Circumstance for a
Mind intended for *Expansion* equal to its Conceptions
which certainly *are great* and extraordinary. I have
repeatedly told you my high Respect for his powers
of Musical Criticism. Alas that one who feels the
Merit of " the MAN " as much every whit as *we* do,
will not do *himself* the Honour of acknowleging it.
It appears to me that we shall save Trouble by bor-
rowing Mr. Jos. Gwilt's Zurich Fugues, as the fewer
References from one book to another the more Time
we shall save, and consequently render the Audi-
tory more Patient. In this Case, perhaps you will
secure the said Book for our Rehearsals To-morrow as well as the Fiddle de dee from Professor
Perkins.

Unless that same Straduarius be Kept in high
Order, I have many doubts of its answering our
Purpose as well as my own tender Stainer; however,
you know me not over given to condemn without a
Hearing.

Forgive my boring you thus, but the Subjects in this Billet seemed to me of some Importance.

Adieu 'till as near 6 as the

Fates will allow,

Yours ever truly,

Turnham Green,
2 o'clock, Friday.

LETTER XVI.

Dec. 9, 1809.

Sir,—I have received the Favour of your Letter, and am obliged to you for the Motive which you express as having actuated you to write it. Had I considered the Controversy (the Introduction of which you seem so much to condemn) as a merely private and personal matter between the two anonymous Antagonists and myself, I should have coincided with you in Opinion that it was not a Subject of sufficient Importance to propose as a prominent Feature in a Lecture; but as the Authors (or Author, for I am inclined to believe the double Signature only a Pretence) attacked not only *myself* but the *whole Body* of Musical Professors together in the most scandalous Style, denominating them no better than a Banditti of Pick-Pockets, I should have considered myself an unworthy Deserter of the Profession to which I belong to suffer it to lie under the base Imputations attributed to them by a malevolent Opponent, when so fair an Opportunity offered itself of confuting his Assertions, and vindicating their Cause : Besides, Sir, if you reflect for a Moment that the Subject I chose for my Lecture was that of " Musical Deception," so flagrant and flagitious an Instance of it came immediately and most naturally within the Scope of my general Design, and I am sure a stronger and more disgraceful Proof of it could not ever be brought forward.

With Regard to " making Amends" for an Act which I cannot consider in the Light of an Offence, you must excuse my differing from you as to its Necessity. That my " recent Conduct" (by which of course you mean my vindication of the Profession assaulted by an anonymous Assassin) should have given cause to " unpleasant Remarks," either " universally " or partially "excited," I am thus far sorry, because I was persuaded in my own mind, not only of the Sincerity of my Intentions to do good by exposing Imposture, but also flattered myself that my Motives would have been as favourably construed as I am conscious that they deserved to be.

Having engaged to read no more than *Six Lectures* in the present Season, the Composition of a supernumerary one would be attended with a Consumption of Time which my very close Pressure of Engagement, I regret to observe, will render impossible.

I remain, with Respect and Gratitude,

Sir,

Your obliged and very Obedient Servant,

To Knight Spenser, Esq.
Surrey Institution.

LETTER XVII.

HUZZA !—Old Wig for ever, and confusion of Face to Pig Tails and Mountebanks !

Chappell at Birchall's tells me that the People teaze his Soul out for the Fugues; that the eternal question is " When does Mr. Wesley intend to bring forward the Fugues in all the twenty-four keys ?" I can plainly perceive that Chappell would be not a little glad to get the Concern into his own and his Master's Hands, but I think we shall be too cunning to suffer that. He says he is convinced that it would be advisable to publish twelve of the first Sett as soon as possible, and he *must* be sincere in this instance I think, because he stopped me yesterday in the Street (when I was very much in haste), and dragged me *vi et Armis* into the Shop to communicate his Complaints.—Now, what say *you* to making a strict revision of the twelve first Preludes and their Correspondent Fugues from my Copy (which you have), and causing them to be transcribed in a capital and correct Manner for the Press without Delay?

" Strike the Iron while 'tis hot" is among the good proverbial Advices, and I see not why we should not take very Advantage *instantly* of the good disposition of the Public, which may by Degrees lead to the solid and permanent establishment of Truth, and over-throw of Ignorance, Prejudice, and Puppyism with regard to our mighty Master.

Chappell has sold 6 numbers of the 2nd, and wants 6 *more directly*, together with *all the Copies* of my Voluntaries printed by Hodsoll which I can rake out for him.

"The Organ is King, be the Blockheads ever so unquiet." I really cannot sufficiently express my Thanks to that Power "which ordereth all Things well" for making me an humble Engine of bringing into due Notice that noble Instrument by which so many Minds are brought to attend to Truths upon which their present and future Happiness depend.

It is also very remarkable (and seems to be providential), that the Contriver of these exquisite Pieces of Art, so calculated to awaken the noblest and most solemn Ideas, should himself have been an exemplary Instance of unaffected Piety, and of the mildest Christian Virtues.

How much additional Value, and what Lustre does it not put upon his Divine Effusions !

"Speed the Plough" must really be the Order of

the Day. Let us remember that we " have put our hand to it," and I think we have no Temptation to " look back."

Let us lose not an Hour in forwarding such Harmony on Earth as has the direct Tendency to bring us to the *Celestial;* and really such Men as Williams and Smith may be considered as Satan's Implements to thwart the Designs of Providence. I do not think I am too severe in this Observation : I assure you I think it the literal Fact.

Write to me about this matter, and by all means crack it about every where how vehement the demand for Bach is *at the most brilliant Music Shop in London.*

I purpose to come from Paddington after the School to you on Saturday Evening, and will endeavour to be with you by 8 o'clock. Adieu.

Wesley

LETTER XVIII.

DEAR FRIEND,—I am in the utmost Distress, and there is no one on Earth but yourself who can help me out of it. Dr. Burney is starke staring mad to hear Sebastian's Sonatas, and I have told him all

how and about your adroit management of his Music
in general. He was immediately resolved on hearing
you 'on the Clavicembalem, and me on the Fiddle
at them. He has appointed *Monday next* at 12
o'clock for our coming to him, as this is the only
time he has left before a second Excursion into the
Country. You see it is an extreme Case. I had
appointed three private Pupils for Monday, but shall
put them all off to Tuesday. Would to Heaven that
you may be able to do the like : The Triumph of
Burney over his own Ignorance and Prejudice is
such a glorious event that surely we ought to make
some sacrifice to enjoy it.

I mentioned young Kollman as quite capable of
playing the Sonatas, but you will see by the enclosed (just received) that he prefers you. Pray com-
ply in this arduous Enterprise. Remember our Cause,
" Good will towards Men " is at the Bottom of it,
and when Sebastian flourishes here, there will be at
least more musical " Peace on Earth."

You see we are utterly ruined unless you come
forward To-morrow.—Think of what we shall have
to announce to the Public; that Dr. Burney (who
has heard almost all the Music of other Folks) should
be listening with Delight at almost 90 years old
to an Author whom he so unknowingly and rashly
had condemned !

Only imagine what an Effect this must have in confounding and putting to Silence such pigmy puerile
Puppies as Williams and Smith and a Farrago of
other such musical Odds and Ends.

I can't dine with you To-morrow, but will breakfast with you at half-past nine, and bring the Sonatas under my Oxster (as the Scots call it), for you will like to have a previous peep. You see I make sure of you on Monday.

I think I see and hear ‚you saying "Yes you may."

Love to all,
Yours (in no Haste as you perceive),

LETTER XIX.

Saturday.

My dear Sir,—Many Thanks for your early and kind Attention.—The Numbers you have sent will be sufficient for my Purpose, as that containing the commencement of the Attack is of the most Importance in the Series of my Cannonade.

We shall have Fun alive next Tuesday, and if you can by Hook or by Crook get J. P. and X.Y.Z. (who I believe one Person) to come, I think I shall have some Murder to answer for, which is a great Comfort to any delicate Conscience. Mrs. Billington has sent me a Letter of Thanks for the Feast on

Wednesday, inviting me to one of the *Alderman* sort
at her House.   Adieu, yours ever,

S Wesley

Turn Over.—Linley writes to say that he will be
glad of his two Books as soon as they can conveni-
ently be sent. If an Opportunity should occur between now and Tuesday, perhaps you can contrive
to get them handed over to him.

LETTER XX.

Sunday, 28 August.

P.S.—I will write to you before Sunday.

MY DEAR SIR,—Many thanks for your kind Attention ; I herewith return a Book which I borrowed on
Friday last as a Compagnon-de-voyage, though he is
not the most flattering Friend in the World. "The
Centaur not fabulous" is among the bitterest of
Religious Satires, and although I believe Dr. Young
might mean to do good by whatever he wrote, there
is always an Asperity of Mind, and a gloomy Cast of
Disposition in the Majority of his Works which seems
to have been the result of either a Saturnine Temper
or some disappointed Passion.

I was certainly in very good Humour for playing
yesterday Evening. I know not whether I was not
put rather upon my mettle by my old Rival's Introduction of his two Critical Companions. That Mr.

Abbot seems to know something about the matter, but I guess that he is one who delights to mix among his Praise " as much Detraction as he can."

Your Man is in haste, which renders me equally so to conclude myself, Dear Sir,

Yours most truly,

P.S.—Mrs. W. desires her kind Respects.

LETTER XXI.

Monday Morning.

MY DEAR SIR,—You must play the Trio, *will ye, nill ye*—so no more on that Subject.

I cannot fix Thursday positively till the Day of our Grand Vocal Rehearsal be settled, and this depends upon Mrs. Vaughan and the Rest of the Lungs to be exerted in the Proof of Sebastian being *no mere Organist.*

I find that the *Cerberus* has been known to say " —Yes,— we allow Bach to be a good Writer for the Organ, but what strange stuff his Attempt at Vocal Music would have been "—!

Yours in Haste.

LETTER XXII.

My DEAR SIR, — You will think me sufficiently stupid in not recollecting when I wrote you last Night, that I have some Intention (if I can but manage it) of coming to you in the course of To-morrow, previous to my mounting the Rostrum ; for as you bespoke me to return to Charlotte Street after *Sermon*, it will be very snug and commodious to put on a Pair of Shoes at so near a distance from the Place of Execution. You see how *ceremonious* I am with my Friends ; and I'll tell you another Secret, which is, that if I feel very hungry, I shall ax for somewhat to eat, look ye, d'ye see? But I cannot appoint my Hour for certain, therefore I insist on your making no Preparation or *Spreadation* for   Yours in Haste,

S. Wesley

LETTER XXIII.

DEAR SIR,—I have the Pleasure to inform you that I have arranged a Plan with Birchall, which will enable me to bring out the 4th Number of the Preludes and Fugues by the 1st of July next, and shall give a Public Notice of it within a few Days hence.

The Subscribers in general have been exceedingly remiss in their Applications for their 3rd Number, which has been one Reason (and the Chief one) for the remaining Book being so long delayed. I was however always resolved at all Hazards to perform my Engagement in this Business with the Public, which I would have much sooner done, could I have coaxed the Engravers into better Humour before.

With best wishes to Mrs. Jacobs and Family,

> I remain,
>> Dear Sir,
>>> Very truly yours,

[signature: Wesley]

Monday,
10 May 1813.

LETTER XXIV.

4, Gower Place,
Euston Square,
Thursday, 15 Feb. 1816.

DEAR SIR,—You are perfectly welcome to the Psalm and Chant annexed if they will suit your purpose: I have also added a few proposals for a Work which, from the Name of the Author, I guess you will find no inclination to decry. My object in publishing it is not emolument, which indeed is

F

seldom to be expected in this Town from any *masterly* musical Productions; but my chief view has been to manifest to English *real* Judges of the Art, how mistaken and false was the Report of those who have Impudently pretended to prove that the great Sebastian Bach could not Compose truly Vocal Music. I mean also that the present Work be regarded as a Study for *Masters* in Orchestral Composition, and such indeed it will be found. I want merely to cover the Expenses of the Publication which I find cannot be done by less than 70 Subscriptions at a Guinea each; at present I have about 40, so that 30 more are required. I need not add much as Panegyric upon any grand Production of the Matchless Man, but I will only just observe that even you, who have been familiar with sundry of his Compositions, will be surprized at some of the gigantic Features of the admirable CREDO in question.

I remain,

Dear Sir,

Sincerely Yours,

My best Respects to Mrs. Jacob.

The Musical Works

OF

SAMUEL WESLEY.

The following is a List of a large Portion of the Compositions of Samuel Wesley.

One vol. of S. Wesley's MSS. now preserved in the British Museum (Add. MSS. 17, 731) is in his own hand-writing, and comprises " MASS, PRO ANGELIS and ANTIPHON EXULTATE DEO." It was presented by the late Mr. Vincent Novello (his esteemed friend), where, as he observes, " it may be carefully preserved for Sam Wesley's sake, after the MS. has been engraved and published to do honour to the memory of the composer." On the first folio is the following :—" *Vincent Novello, Craven Hill Cottage, Bayswater.*—Presented by him for preservation in the musical library of the British Museum, as a tribute of respect and a token of veneration for the memory of his beloved friend, Samuel Wesley, who, in the donor's estimation, was one of the greatest musical geniuses that England has ever produced.—May Morning, 1849.

" Both these autograph compositions, neither of which has yet been published (as they ought long since to have been, for the gratification of all those of his brother musicians, who are competent to judge of the superior skill displayed by the composer in their mode of construction), are masterpieces of counterpoint."

(In fol. 2 of " *Gloria in excelsis Deo,*") Mr. Novello states that " this manuscript contains the whole Gregorian Mass " Pro Angelis " (except the " *Kyrie,*" which is already published in Novello's ' Sacred Music,' dedicated to the Rev. Wm. V. Fryer). It is arranged and harmonized by Samuel Wesley, and this copy is in his own hand-writing. I prize this MS. the more highly from its having been kindly presented to me by the widow of my beloved friend Charles Stokes, after his death in 1839. Vincent Novello, 69, Dean Street, Soho Square."

On folio 27, " Antiphona," is the following written in red pencil :—" Composed by my dear friend, Sam Wesley, 1800. It is a most masterly piece of vocal counterpoint, and this fine copy of it the more valuable in my estimation from being in the Composer's own hand-writing.—Vincent Novello."

Six Voluntaries for the Organ. Op. 6. Book 1. Do., Book 2. (Pub. by Purday.)

Twelve short pieces for the Organ, with full Voluntary added, inscribed to Performers on the Seraphine and Organists in general. (Pub. by Green.)

Six Introductory Movements for the Organ, to which is added a loud Voluntary. (Pub. by Clementi.)

Voluntary for the Organ, inscribed to Thomas Attwood—(this is in B flat). (Pub. by Purday.)

Do., inscribed to William Linley. (Pub. by Monro and May.) (This is in G minor).

Do., inscribed to H. I. Gauntlett. Do. (in G).

A short and familiar Voluntary for the Organ, in A. (Purday).

A Voluntary for the Organ, in D; inscribed to Wm. Drummer. (Pub. by Willis.)

Chorus " Glory be to the Father," from the anthem " I will take heed;" with a short biographical notice of S. Wesley. (Pub. by Novello. Cathedral Voluntaries, No. 10.)

Verse and Chorus, " We believe that Thou shalt come ;" from the Service in F. (Do., No 26.)

Do., " For the Lord is gracious." (Do., No. 28.)

Parochial Psalm Tunes and Interludes. (Only Book 1, pub. by Willis.)

Characteristic Airs for the Seraphine, Nos. 4, 5, 6. (Pub. by Green.)

God Save the King ; with verse by *Charles Wesley*, the brother of *Samuel* (Birchall.)

The Sicilian Mariner's Hymn, by Do. (Birchall.)

Sanctus in E flat, by Do. Do., Perhaps it is not Love ; words by Shenstone, music by Charles Wesley.

O worship the Lord, by Do.

When Delia, by Do.

Glee, 3 v., " Now I know." Do.

By *Samuel Wesley*, " Father of Light ;" words from Thomson's " Seasons ;" for four voices. [This is one of dear Sam's most charming compositions.] (Pub. by the Regent's Harmonic Institution, Argyle Rooms.)

Three Hymns (from the Fitzwilliam Library, Cambridge), composed by Handel ; arranged in score by S. Wesley. (Goulding and Co.)

National Song, " Looking o'er the Moonlight ;" adapted to a favourite air by S. W. (Purday.)

" True Blue and Old England ;" composed by S. Wesley. (Willis.)

The following is (in one volume, bound) headed—" List of Pianoforte Music by Samuel Wesley." The whole of this fine collection of compositions, which are as beautiful as they are (now unfortunately become) rare, are in the possession of my esteemed friend, Mr. Thomas Hawkins. 1849 :—

Grand Duett in three movements, for the Pianoforte ; inscribed to Fred. Marshall, of Leamington. (Lonsdale.) *N.B.*—This was composed expressly for Vincent Novello to perform with S. Wesley, at the Portuguese Chapel in South Grosvenor Square, on which fine organ they have often played.

Du. March in D, No. 25. (Hodsoll.)

Pastorelli's Polacca in G, Rondo. (A. Novello.)

Sonata, with Fugue on a subject by Salomon ; inscribed to Mrs. Oom, in D minor. (Birchall.)

A Fugue for the Pianoforte ; inscribed to Logier. (Willis.)

Introduction and Air in G ; inscribed to Mrs. Stirling. (Willis.)

Rondo for the Pianoforte, in G. (Mori and Lavenu.)

Introduction and Waltz in D. (Alex. Lee, Quadrant.)

Grand Coronation March in D. (Willis.)

Var. on an Italian Air in F ; inscribed to Rev. Archdeacon Nares. (Mori.)

A Favourite Air in G, by Weber (Freyschutz); to Miss Burgh (Birchall.)

Polish Air in D minor; to the Duchess of Bedford. (Birchall.)

Du. in La Cora Rasu, in C. (Birchall.)

The Widow Waddle, in A; inscribed to Mr. Grimaldi. (Button and Whittaker.)

Purcell's Air, "I attempt from Love's sickness," in A; to Wm. Linley. (A. Novello.)

The Christmas Carol, in E minor. (Clementi.)

Old English Air, "Kitty Alone," in G minor; to Jos. Street. (Novello.)

"Scots, wha ha'e," in B flat. (Birchall.)

The Deserter's Meditation; to the Misses Harrison, in F. (Chappell.)

The Bay of Biscay, inscribed to Clementi, in B. flat. (Monro and May.)

Orphan Mary, in B flat. (Hodsoll.)

The following are in *manuscript* in Mr. Hawkins' book: —

Hornpipe and Vari., in D. [I remember hearing S. Wesley play this Hornpipe—which, like all his compositions has a remarkably fine bass to it—as a part of his admirable Organ Concerto in D, which still remains unpublished. I have presented the original score for preservation in the musical library of the British Museum.—V. Novello.]

Air in Tekeli in G.

Divertimentos, consisting of an Adagio, a March, and a Waltz, in C.

Moll Pately, as a Rondo in F. See *Addison's Spectator*, No. 67.

Old Towler (air by Shield), in D.

"Off she Goes," in D.

Irish Melody—"Fly not yet," in F,

Patty Kavannah (Irish Melody), in C.

"Bellissima Signora" (Air by M. P. King), as a Rondo in B flat.

Lady Mary Douglas, in D.

The Lass of Richmond Hill in B flat.

Sweet Enslaver (Air by L. Atterbury), with Variations.

The following List is taken from the *Musical World*, 1837.

Te Deum, Jubilate, Sanctus, Kyrie Eleison, Nunc Dimittis, and Burial Service.

"A Confitebor:" containing Solos, Duets, Trios, Choruses, &c., with full Orchestral Accompaniments.

"An Ode to St. Cecilia's Day:" the words by the Rev. Samuel Wesley, formerly Rector of Epworth, Lincolnshire, containing Solos, Duets, Quartets, Choruses, &c., with full Orchestral Accompaniments.

"Missa Solemnis." A Grand Mass, every movement of which is founded on a Gregorian phrase which runs throughout the composition.

"In Exitu Israel," a Choral Motett for eight voices, performed at the Hereford Festival, the score added by his son Mr. S. S. Wesley.

"Exultate Deo:" a Choral Motett for five voices, performed at the Birmingham and Worcester Festivals, the score by the Composer, with additional Accompaniments by his Son, Mr. S. S. Wesley.

Choral Motetts :—Dixit Dominus.
Omnia Vanitas.
Tu es Sacerdos.
Te decet Hymnus.
Hosanna in Excelsis.

"Funeral Anthem," composed on the death of his Brother, Mr. Charles Wesley. (Novello.)

Anthem : "I am well pleased," published in Page's Harmonia Sacra.

Anthem : "Behold how good a thing," with Organ Obligato Accompaniment.

Motett : "Domine Salvum fac Reginam," with Organ Obligato, in Novello's Collection.

Six Hundred Chorales or Psalm Tunes, or more.

Many Motetts, Anthems, Solos, in MS., too numerous to particularize.

Grand Duet for the Organ, published by Lonsdale. This is (as a whole) the greatest composition for the Organ which has appeared since the days of Sebastian Bach.

A Second Grand Organ Duet, unpublished. The composer preferred this to the other, and considered it his best composition for the Organ.

Preludes and Fugues, or Exercises for the Organ. Goulding.

Concerto for the Organ, on the Air " Rule Britannia."

Concerto for the Organ in G.

Concerto for the Organ in D.

Voluntary in D.
    Ditto   in C.
    Ditto   in C minor.
    Ditto   in G.
    Ditto   in D.
    Ditto   in C.
    Ditto   in E flat.
    Ditto   in D.
    Ditto   in G minor.
    Ditto   in F.
    Ditto   in A.
    Ditto   in F.

Grand Fugue, dedicated to W. Drummer, Esq. (Willis.) This is a beautiful composition, and contains the March from the Overture to the " Ode to St. Cecilia's Day."

Three Voluntaries, dedicated to Mr. Harding.

A second set ditto do. (Coventry and Hollier.) The last Fugue in this set is most lovely.

Twelve Short Pieces, to which is added a Grand Fugue, composed at the request of Muzio Clementi. (Collard & Co.)

Six Introductory Movements or Soft Voluntaries, to which is added a Fugue in D. (Collard & Co.)

A Book of Interludes for Young Organists. (Coventry & Hollier.)

Rondo from an Organ Concerto. (R. H. Institution.)

Trio for Pianoforte and Two Flutes. (Novello.)

Fugue in D. (Novello.)

Easy Voluntaries. (D'Almaine.)

Sonatina, inscribed to Miss Meeking. (Goulding.)

Three Sonatas, dedicated to the Hon. Misses Lamb.

Sonatas for the Pianoforte, à quatre mains.

The " Siege of Badajoz," containing a fine March in D. Preston.

Divertimento. Dedicated to Miss Walker.

Rondo on " Will Putty."

Waltz, The Sky Rocket.

" Behold where Dryden." Bass Scena. Poetry by Gray.

The House that Jack Built. (Monro.)

Concerto for Piano.

Ditto for three Pianos.

The Autophagos.

Election Squib.

Many Arrangements of Handel's.

Songs and Choruses by Handel, Beethoven, &c. &c. Canzonets, Songs, Duets, Glees, Gregorians, Fugues, Voluntaries, Anacreontic and Table Songs, &c. &c., in MS.

——

" Oratorio of Ruth," composed by my father between the ages of *six* and *eight*.

A copy of this was presented to Dr. Boyce. The original manuscript, bound, is in my possession. with the following statement written on the first page by his Father, the Rev. Charles Wesley:—" This Oratorio was composed by Samuel Wesley, when eight years of age, never having been taught music or composition, and many of y^e airs completed when only six years old."

CHALONER & COOKE, Printers, Oxford Arms Passage, St. Paul's, E.C.

www.ingramcontent.com/pod-product-compliance
Lightning Source LLC
Chambersburg PA
CBHW022151020726
47496CB00008B/2665